The
Comanche Indians

by Bill Lund

Reading Consultant:
John Wauqua
Education Department
Comanche Tribal Council

Bridgestone Books
an Imprint of Capstone Press

Bridgestone Books are published by Capstone Press
818 North Willow Street, Mankato, Minnesota 56001
Copyright © 1997 by Capstone Press
Printed in the United States of America

Library of Congress Cataloging-in-Publication Data
Lund, Bill, 1954-
    The Comanche Indians/by Bill Lund.
        p. cm.--(Native peoples)
    Includes bibliographical references and index.
    Summary: Provides an overview of the past and present lives of the
Comanches, covering their daily life, customs, relations with the
government and others, and more.
    ISBN 1-56065-478-3
    1. Comanche Indians--Juvenile literature. [1. Comanche Indians.
2. Indians of North America.]   I. Title. II. Series: Lund, Bill, 1954-
Native peoples.
E99.C85L86   1997
973'.049745--dc21

                                        96-39766
                                        CIP
                                        AC

Photo credits
FPG, 16; Lee Kuhn, 20
Index Stock/Dan Abernathy, 6; Barry Levy, 18
International Stock/George Ancona, cover
Western History Collections, University of Oklahoma Library, 8, 10, 12, 14

Table of Contents

Map

Canada

U.S.A.

Mexico

Where the Comanche used to live

Fast Facts

Today many Comanche Indians live like most other North Americans. In the past, they practiced a different way of life. Their food, homes, and clothes helped make them special. These facts tell how the Comanche once lived.

Food: Comanches ate buffalo meat. They also ate the meat from other animals they hunted. They gathered fruits and vegetables from the land.

Home: They lived in tepees. Tepees were made of poles. The poles were covered with animal skins.

Clothing: Comanche men wore breechcloths. This was a piece of deerskin. It passed between the legs. It was tied with a belt. In winter, men wore robes and high boots. Women wore loose, long-sleeved dresses. These dresses were often decorated with fringe and beads.

Language: Comanches spoke their own Comanche language.

Past Location: Comanches controlled a large area of land. It covered Texas, New Mexico, Oklahoma, Colorado, and Kansas.

Current Location: Today most Comanches live in Oklahoma and Texas.

Special Events: Comanches hold powwows to honor their beliefs. They dance and sing at powwows.

The Comanche Indians

The Comanche were once known for being skilled warriors. A warrior is a brave fighter. The Comanches today live a peaceful life with their neighbors. They do not have a reservation. A reservation is land set aside for use by Native Americans. Many Comanches live in Oklahoma and Texas.

Before European settlers came, Comanches ruled large areas of land. They lived by hunting. They were great warriors and horse riders.

The Comanches fought hard to keep their lands. They also fought for their freedom. They tried to keep their way of life alive.

Today many Comanches still honor their old way of life. They hold powwows. A powwow is a gathering for all Comanches. During powwows, they dance and sing. This honors Comanche beliefs. Powwows help the Comanche people remember their great history.

Many Comanches live in Oklahoma and Texas.

Tepees and Buffalo

Long ago, Comanche people traveled over great areas of land. They did not build lasting homes. Sometimes they would take a break from traveling. Then they would set up a camp.

Comanches had special houses called tepees. A tepee was made of poles. The poles formed a cone-shaped triangle. Animal skins were stretched over the poles. Tepees were perfect for traveling. They could easily be taken down and set up again.

Buffalo was an important Comanche food. They ate buffalo meat all year long. The meat was dried. That way it did not spoil. Pemmican was a popular food. This was dried meat pounded into powder. It was mixed with berries and melted fat.

Comanches used other parts of the buffalo, too. They made buffalo horns into bowls and cups. Comanches shaped buffalo bones into tools. Buffalo skin was made into clothes and tepee coverings. Buffalo hair was made into brushes.

Comanches once lived in houses called tepees.

Great Hunters

In the past, Comanches lived by hunting. People moved around looking for buffalo to hunt. If buffalo were nearby, they would set up camp. The men would hunt. Comanche men were known for their great hunting skills.

The Comanches had small hunting groups. Each man hunted for his family's food. Hunting was best during the end of fall. At that time, buffalo were fat for winter. Their coats were thicker, too.

When men were too old to hunt, they helped others. They made hunting weapons. A weapon is something that can be used in a fight. It can be used to attack or protect.

Comanches mainly hunted with bows and arrows. Sometimes they used lances. A lance has a long handle and a pointed end. Usually, weapons were made out of wood. Sometimes Comanches carved animal bones into weapons.

Comanches used to hunt buffalo.

Quanah Parker
Chief of the Comanch

Skilled Horse Riders

Spanish settlers brought horses to North America in the 1600s. This changed the Comanche way of life forever.

With horses, Comanches could travel further. They could hunt animals that were far away. They could bring food back to the camp.

Soon the Comanches became known for being excellent horse riders. Men, women, and children all learned to ride horses. The Comanche people were travelers. Most of their lives were spent on horseback.

Comanches even learned how to catch wild horses. They waited until the horses were drinking. Then they surrounded the horses. They tried to catch horses when they were full of water. This made the horses slower and easier to capture.

Comanches were known as excellent horse riders.

Bands

The Comanches are divided into different groups. In the past, each group's life was different. It depended on where the group lived. The groups were called bands.

Most people in a band were family. People could leave their band if they wanted. Then they joined another band.

Each band had its own leaders. One leader was called the peace chief. He was an older, respected Comanche. His job was to help people with their problems.

Sometimes the Comanches went to war. Then the bands also chose a war chief. The war chief was a respected fighter. During the war, he would rule his band.

The band council was another ruling group. All the men in the band were members of the council. The council decided when to go to war. They also decided where to hunt.

Each Comanche band was ruled by a chief.

Comanche History

The Comanches used to live in an area called the Comancheria. Comancheria means "the land of the Comanche." The Comancheria covered Texas, New Mexico, Oklahoma, Colorado, and Kansas.

The Comanches had to fight to keep their land. Other Indian groups wanted it. European settlers wanted it, too. After a lot of fighting, the U.S. government took their land. It forced the Comanche onto one reservation.

Reservation life was hard for Comanches. They were not allowed to hunt for food. The government tried to change them. Many Comanches would not give up their beliefs or language. They fought to keep their way of life.

After 40 years, the government decided to close the reservation. It gave small pieces of land to Comanches. But it was still hard to make a living. Crops did not grow well on the land.

Reservation life was hard for Comanches.

Comanche Art

Comanches valued their weapons highly. Weapons were used for hunting and war. This is why Comanches often decorated them.

Comanches made covers for their weapons. The covers were made from animal skins. They were decorated with feathers or deer hooves. Sometimes beads were used.

Comanches also made shields. A shield is carried to protect the body from an attack. Sometimes the shields were painted.

Comanches made paints from clay and plants. They also painted tepee covers and other animal skins. Sometimes they painted animal bones. Most Comanche paintings were of battles or hunts. The paintings showed riding warriors shooting bows and arrows.

The Comanches also made beaded necklaces. They made feather decorations for their hair.

Comanches made beaded necklaces.

Why the Comanche Left

At one time, Comanches were part of Idaho's Shoshone Indians. But in the 1700s, Comanches left the Shoshone. They became their own group. Comanches tell stories about why they left the Shoshone. Here is one of those stories.

One day, two bands were hunting together. After a long hunt, a bear was killed. The bands wanted to know who killed the bear. The warrior who had would receive great honor.

Two warriors said that they had killed the bear. Each warrior was from a different band.

People could not decide who shot the arrow. They did not know who told the truth. The people sided with the warrior from their own band. They argued.

The bands could not agree. So they split up. The band that became the Comanche moved south. The Shoshone band did not move.

Two bands argued over who had killed the bear.

Hands On: Play Shinny

Shinny was a popular game among many Native Americans. The Comanche Indians formed teams to play this game. You will need two or more people to play shinny.

What You Need

One tennis ball
Baseball bats (one for each player)
Masking tape

What You Do

1. Divide players into two teams. Choose one person to be the scorekeeper.
2. Tear off two long pieces of tape. Place the tape on each end of your playing area. The pieces of tape are each team's goal line.
3. Place the ball in the middle of the playing area.
4. Stand behind your team's piece of tape.
5. The scorekeeper gives the signal to start.
6. At the signal, run onto the playing area. Use the bat to hit the ball past the other team's goal line.
7. Your team scores one point when the ball passes the other team's goal line. The scorekeeper keeps track of the points. The winning team is the one who scores the most points.

Words to Know

comancheria (koh-MAN-cher-ee-ah)—the area where the Comanche once lived; it covered Texas, New Mexico, Oklahoma, Colorado, and Kansas.

lance (LANSS)—a weapon with a long handle and a pointed end

powwow (POW-wow)—a gathering for Native Americans

reservation (rez-ur-VAY-shuhn)—land set aside for use by Native Americans

tepee (TEE-pee)—a house made of poles that are covered by animal skins

Read More

Alter, Judy. *The Comanches*. New York: Franklin Watts, 1994.

Mooney, Martin J. *The Comanche Indians*. New York: Chelsea House, 1993.

Rollings, Willard. *The Comanche*. New York: Chelsea House, 1989.

Useful Addresses

National Museum of the American Indian
Smithsonian Institution
Washington, DC 20560

Comanche Tribal Council
HC 32, Box 908
Lawton, OK 73502

Internet Sites

Codetalk Home Page
http://www.codetalk.fed.us/home.html

Native American Indian
http://indy4.fdl.cc.mn.us/~isk/

Index